NATURAL WORLD

KOALA

HABITATS • LIFE CYCLES • FOOD CHAINS • THREATS

Michael Leach

RAINTREE
STECK-VAUGHN
PUBLISHERS

A Harcourt Company

Austin   New York
www.raintreesteckvaughn.com

NATURAL WORLD

Black Rhino • Chimpanzee • Crocodile • Dolphin • Elephant • Giant Panda
Giraffe • Golden Eagle • Gorilla • Great White Shark • Grizzly Bear
Hippopotamus • Killer Whale • Koala • Leopard • Lion • Orangutan
Penguin • Polar Bear • Tiger • Wolf • Zebra

Cover: A koala, up close
Title page: A koala eating eucalyptus leaves
Contents page: The koala's powerful grip can cling on to
vertical tree trunks even when feeding
Index page: A koala resting on a branch

Published by Raintree Steck-Vaughn Publishers,
an imprint of Steck-Vaughn Company

Library of Congress Cataloging-in-Publication Data
Leach, Michael.
    Koala: habitats, life cycles, food chains, threats / Michael Leach
        p. cm.—(Natural World)
    Summary: Presents information on the physical characteristics,
behavior, habitat, and life cycle of the koala, a nocturnal marsupial
found only in Australia.
    Includes bibliographical references (p.).
    ISBN 0-7398-5230-2
    1. Koala—Juvenile literature. [1. Koala.] I. Title. II. Natural world
(Austin, Tex.)

QL737.M384 L42 2002
599.2'5—dc21   2001059171

Printed in Italy. Bound in the United States.

1 2 3 4 5 6 7 8 9 0 LB 06 05 04 03 02

Picture acknowledgments
Bruce Coleman Collection 22; *Corbis* 15 Yann-Arthus Bertrand, 17 O
Alamany and E Vicens, 19 Michael J Yamashita, 39 Richard Glover,
42 Wolfgang Kaehler, 45 middle Yann-Arthus Bertrand; *FLPA* front
cover Minden pictures, 3 Gerard Lacz, 6 Martin B Withers, 7 David
Hosking, 8 RP Lawrence, 16 Gerard Lacz, 18 Eric Woods, 20 Jurgen
and Christine Sohns, 21 W Wisniewski, 25 Gerard Lacz, 26 Gerard
Lacz, 27 David Hosking, 29 Mark Newman, 32 Silvestris, 36 Gerard
Lacz, 37 W Meinderts/Foto Natura, 38 Eric and David Hosking, 41
Minden Pictures, 43 Silvestris, 45 bottom Gerard Lacz, 48 Terry
Whittaker; *NHPA* 1 Gerard Lacz, 9 Dave Watts, 11 ANT, 12 ANT, 13
ANT, 23 ANT, 28 ANT, 31 Gerard Lacz, 33 Gerard Lacz, 34 Rich
Kirchner, 35 ANT, 44 middle ANT, 44 bottom ANT; *OSF* 14 Daniel J
Cox, 45 top Danial J Cox; *Still Pictures* 10 Roland Seitre, 40 Roland
Seitre, 44 top Roland Seitre. Artwork by Michael Posen.

Contents

Meet the Koala

Koalas are furry animals that live only in Australia, and only in trees. In fact they live only in certain types of trees, called eucalyptus trees, where they eat the leaves. A koala can walk and even run on the ground, but it only comes down when it needs to move from one tree to another, to find fresh food.

AUSTRALIA

AUSTRALIA

▲ The red shading shows where koalas live, in the eucalyptus woodlands of the eastern side of Australia. The inset map shows where Australia is.

KOALA FACTS

A full-grown male koala weighs up to 26 lbs. (12 kg) and measures about 28 in. (70 cm) from nose to tail. An adult female weighs up to 18 lbs. (8 kg) and measures about 26 in. (65 cm) from nose to tail.

●

The koala's scientific name is *Phascolarctos cinereus*, which means "ash-colored pouch bear."

●

Koalas are members of the group of animals called marsupials. This name comes from the Latin word *marsupium*, meaning "pouch."

Nose
The koala has a very good sense of smell. The nose looks like bare skin but it is covered with very fine hairs.

Ear
Big, furry, pale-fringed ears provide keen hearing.

Fur
Koalas live out in the open, on tree branches. Thick, waterproof fur protects them against rain and too much heat or cold.

Pouch
Only the female koala has a pouch, where her baby lives while it is young. The pouch is hidden from view on the front of her lower body. Whatever the weather outside, the pouch is always warm and protected.

Limbs
The koala climbs with its body upright, holding on by its arms and legs. Long, strong thigh muscles make its legs more powerful than most other animals of its size.

Claws
Long, sharp claws press into and grip the bark and branches.

▲ An adult koala

Habitat

Koalas are highly specialized to survive only in one type of habitat. This is woodland with plenty of eucalyptus trees, also known as gum trees. They provide the koala with food, water, safety from ground predators, and all other needs. Koalas do not have dens, tree-holes, or nests. They sleep, eat, and breed on the branches.

► Red River gum trees, one of the species of eucalyptus that provide koalas with both food and shelter.

NOT A "BEAR"

When Europeans first explored Australia, they thought the koala was a kind of monkey or sloth. Then they decided it was a type of bear, and it became known as the "koala bear." But the koala is not related to bears. It is in a very different group of mammals, the marsupials.

Life in the Trees

Koalas are light gray or light brown, with speckles or dapples on their rear end. These colors give good camouflage and make the koala very difficult to see among leaves. The koala is a slow but strong climber and usually moves with its body upright. It descends from a tree backward, by "reversing" down the trunk. Koalas have excellent balance and do not fall, even when asleep. They are mainly nocturnal. They doze high in trees by day, and become active at night.

▲ The koalas' appearance and behavior were very different from anything ever seen by early European settlers in Australia.

▲ The red-necked wallaby is one of the marsupials still found throughout much of Australia.

Relatives

Koalas are marsupials. They are furry, warm-blooded, and feed their babies on milk—just like other mammals. But a female marsupial has a special feature, which other mammals lack: a pocket-like pouch on her front. After her baby is born, it crawls into the pouch and stays there, feeding on her milk. A newborn marsupial is extremely small and not well developed.

Long ago, marsupials were found across the world. But gradually other kinds of mammals took over. However, Australia has been a huge island, separated from other lands, for about 45 million years. Over this vast time period, many kinds of marsupials have survived there, and evolved or changed. This is why Australian animals are so different from animals in other parts of the world.

▲ There are three species of wombat in Australia. This is a common wombat with young coming out from an underground den.

Today there are about 260 kinds, or species, of marsupials. They range from tiny shrew-sized creatures weighing as little as 3 grams to huge red kangaroos. Other marsupials include wallabies, bandicoots, and opossums. Marsupials are found mainly in Australia and Southeast Asia, with some in South America and a few in Central and North America.

CLOSEST RELATION

The koala's closest living relative is another marsupial with a vaguely bear-like shape, but a very different lifestyle. This is the ground-dwelling, fast-digging wombat.

A Koala Is Born

SHORT PREGNANCY

A joey is born about 35 days after the female has mated.

▼ A newborn koala inside its mother's pouch.

A young koala is called a joey. It is born in the branches of a tree, high above the ground. The young koala is tiny, about the size of a grape. It weighs only half a gram. It cannot see and has no hair. Its ears have not yet developed. But its sense of smell is very good.

The newborn joey uses its strong front legs to "swim" through its mother's thick fur. Guided by smell, it crawls into the mother's pouch. Inside are two teats (nipples) where the mother's milk is released. The joey fixes onto one of them and grips tightly. The end of the teat enlarges inside the joey's mouth, so the joey cannot fall off.

▲ By the age of 24 weeks, the joey can see and move around easily.

Upside-Down Pouch

Many female marsupials, such as kangaroos, have a pouch that opens on the upper side, like a pocket. But the koala's pouch opens at the lower side. Its entrance is near the mother's tail. Once the joey is inside, the pouch entrance closes. The joey is warm and protected, with plenty of milk to drink. Its mother can still move easily through the treetops.

Life in the Pouch

The joey (baby koala) grows very slowly inside the pouch. Its eyes open about 22 weeks after birth. For the first time, the joey pokes its head through the pouch entrance and looks around. There are muscles around the pouch entrance, like the drawstring on a purse. The mother can tighten these to close the entrance and stop the baby from falling out.

▲ At 6 months old, the joey spends a lot of time looking out of its mother's pouch.

12

A Change of Diet

Until now the joey has fed only on its mother's milk. Shortly after its eyes open, it starts to eat "pap." These are special droppings produced by the mother, made from eucalyptus leaves she has partly digested. The baby's stomach cannot digest fresh leaves, which are very tough. But pap contains leaves that the mother's stomach has begun to break down. They are in a form that the joey can digest.

Pap is the first step toward a life of eating leaves. But the young koala still takes milk from its mother's teat every day. On milk alone, the joey grows slowly. Once it begins to eat pap, growth is much faster.

FUR AND TEETH

At about 24 weeks old, the joey has fur all over its body, and its first teeth begin to appear.

▶ This joey is suckling while its mother rests on a branch.

Out of the Pouch

At 6 months old, the joey leaves the safety of its pouch for the first time. It is now about 8 in. (20 cm) long and weighs nearly 18 oz. (500 g). It keeps very close to its mother and returns to the pouch within a few minutes. Gradually the outings become longer. While the joey is out, the mother licks the pouch clean.

▲ After first leaving the pouch, the joey stays close to the entrance, ready to dart back in at any sign of danger.

At first the young koala keeps within touching distance of its mother. It returns to the pouch to sleep and if danger threatens. As the youngster grows stronger, it practices climbing skills and explores farther.

Piggyback Rides

At 9 months old, the joey weighs 2.2 lbs. (1 kg). It is now too big for the pouch and rides on its mother's back. Joey and mother keep in contact among the leaves by soft squeaks and hums. If the joey wanders too far, the mother grunts angrily to summon it back.

The joey is weaned at around 10 months, but stays near its mother for another two. By the time a year has passed, the mother may have mated again and have another joey growing in her pouch.

▼ The joey soon learns to cling to its mother's fur and ride on her back. This keeps the youngster safe and allows the adult to climb easily around the trees.

Learning to Survive

At about 1 year old, the young koala leaves its mother to begin adult life. First it must find a new home. Koalas do not stay together, apart from mother and baby, or when a female and male mate. They are solitary (live alone). Every adult has its own area of woodland, known as a home range. It stays in this range, where it has both food and shelter.

Some home ranges overlap with the home ranges of other koalas. Male koalas do not usually mind females in the area, provided they do not come too close (except when breeding). Likewise, females tolerate males. But a koala is likely to attack another adult of the same sex if it comes too near.

◀ After leaving its mother, a young koala must quickly find its own feeding territory or it will starve.

▶ A sleepy koala on Philip Island wakes up in a tree in his home range.

ONE KOALA PER TREE

It is very rare for two koalas to eat or sleep in the same tree, no matter how big the tree is. One usually drives the other away.

Leaving Home

If a joey tries to stay with its mother, the mother may drive it away—particularly if she has another baby inside her pouch. A young male koala must be especially careful. If it stays with its mother too long, it will be viciously chased by the local dominant (chief) male, and perhaps injured.

A New Home

A young koala may have to travel some distance
to find a new home range. This can be risky. A
koala cannot jump between branches, like a
monkey. It comes down to the ground and walks.
It sniffs the bottom of each trunk, to find out if the
tree is the right kind to provide food, and for the
scents of other koalas in the area.

The year-old koala is still small, less than one-third
of its full-grown size. The search for a new home
is a dangerous time. The koala's main predators
live on the ground (as shown on page 20), so the
youngster must find a new place quickly.

▲ Koalas are slow
and clumsy on the
ground. This is the
time when they are
most likely to be
attacked by enemies.

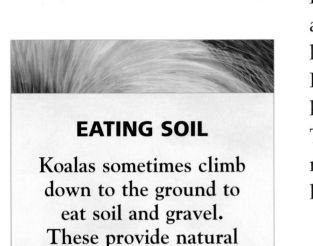

EATING SOIL

Koalas sometimes climb down to the ground to eat soil and gravel. These provide natural minerals and help to break up the tough leaves inside the koala's stomach.

If a young adult tries to move into an already crowded area, there may be a lack of food and even fights over trees. If it finds an area with very few other koalas, it has little chance of breeding. The best answer is a home range that is not occupied and that also has other koalas nearby.

▼ A koala sniffs the base of a tree, searching for the scent of other koalas. It may also have climbed down to eat some soil from the ground.

Enemies

Most koalas are killed on the ground. Their enemies include foxes, dingoes, quolls (native cats), large snakes, domestic dogs, and occasionally even pet cats. A koala cornered by a large predator in the open, away from trees, has little chance. It may lash out with its front paws, and the long claws can badly hurt an enemy. This sometimes drives away smaller predators.

When frightened, a koala can run surprisingly fast for a short distance. If it makes it to a tree, the koala will jump from the ground onto the trunk. Pushing hard with its strong back legs, it soon disappears into the branches.

▼ Dingoes are Australia's largest predators. They are powerful hunters that eagerly kill and eat any koala found walking on the ground.

► With huge, strong talons, a wedge-tailed eagle can easily pull an unsuspecting young koala from high in a tree.

But even in trees, young koalas are at risk from big birds of prey such as large owls and wedge-tailed eagles. These swoop down to pluck them from the branches. Adult koalas are too big for these birds to kill.

Fires

Forest and bush fires are common in the hot, dry Australian summer. Eucalyptus trees are particularly at risk because their leaves contain oils that burn well and spread the fire quickly. This is one of the koala's greatest threats. It is not fast enough to escape the flames.

▲ Koalas can stay balanced in the fork of a tree even when fast asleep.

Daily Routine

Once a young koala has found a home range, it will probably stay there for the rest of its life—particularly if it is a female. The young adult begins the slow routine that it will follow day after day, for years. It is most active around dusk and dawn, and feeds mainly in the early part of the night. It sleeps by day, although a male koala sometimes feeds during the day.

In cool weather, the koala sleeps curled into a tight ball, to keep in body warmth. In hot weather it lies draped over a branch, to let a cooling breeze blow around its legs and body. Koalas do not sweat, but they may lick themselves. As the spit dries, it draws heat from the body—in the same way that our own sweat keeps us cool.

During the day, the koala wakes occasionally to groom its fur or change position. In hot weather it moves into the shade. On cool days it looks for a sunny, warm branch.

▼ Koalas spend part of every day licking their fur to keep it clean.

23

Finding Food

Koalas are one of the most specialized feeders in the animal world. They eat mainly, or even only, eucalyptus leaves. They sometimes try leaves from other trees, such as acacia, oak, mistletoe, and box. But these make up only a tiny part of the diet. A koala identifies these different types of food by smell.

▼ Koalas' main predators are dingoes, large owls, and wedge-tailed eagles.

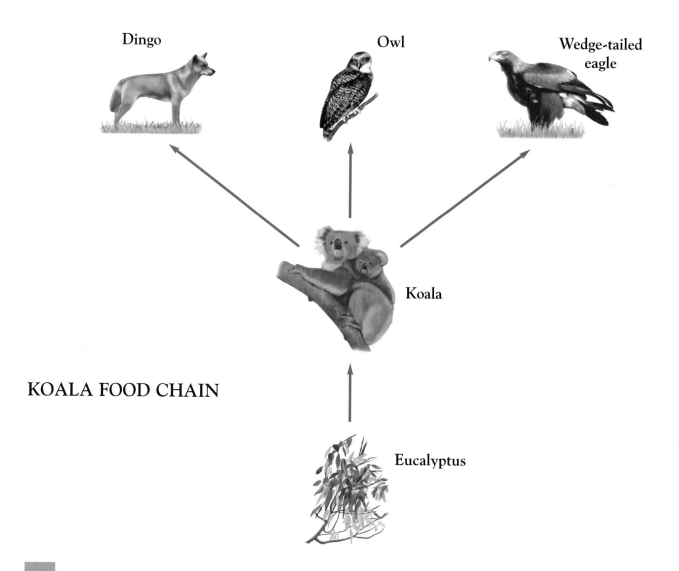

Dingo

Owl

Wedge-tailed eagle

Koala

KOALA FOOD CHAIN

Eucalyptus

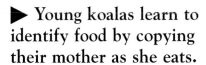 Young koalas learn to identify food by copying their mother as she eats.

Fussy Eaters

A single koala may eat just two types of eucalyptus all of its life. This is partly because it does not like to change. Once a young koala starts to eat the leaves of the trees in its home range, it tries to feed on the same kinds, year after year. It ignores unfamiliar types of eucalyptus, even though they may be perfectly good for eating, and koalas in other places thrive on them.

Each region of Australia has its own types of eucalyptus, and most woodlands contain only a few of these. So koalas in the northeast eat different kinds of eucalyptus leaves than those in the southeast.

Feeding

A hungry koala first finds a safe place to sit. Extra-thick fur on its rear end acts as a soft cushion for sitting on hard branches. The koala eats nearby leaves first, moving its head around. Then it leans or stretches its body, and pulls twigs and branches with its front paws, to reach other leaves. The koala carefully sniffs every leaf. Young leaves near the branch tips contain a chemical called prussic acid. This is a very dangerous poison that can kill a koala that eats too much of it. If the koala smells this acid, it avoids the leaf.

◀ A koala uses its sharp front teeth to nip through the stem of leaf.

The koala's very sharp incisor (front) teeth bite through the leaf stems. Then the large molar (back) teeth cut, slice, and chew them. A wide gap between the front and back teeth allows the thick, tough, leathery leaves to move around inside the mouth, so they are thoroughly chopped and softened.

The koala's stretchy cheeks can expand to form big pouches. Sometimes a koala stores unchewed leaves in its cheeks, and then moves to a safer or more comfortable place to chew them.

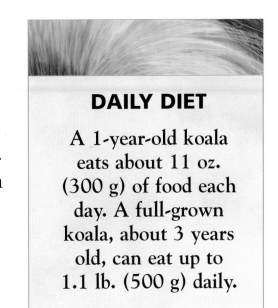

DAILY DIET

A 1-year-old koala eats about 11 oz. (300 g) of food each day. A full-grown koala, about 3 years old, can eat up to 1.1 lb. (500 g) daily.

▼ A koala can carry a lot of food in its mouth by filling the elastic-like skin pouches that form its cheeks.

Poisonous Food

Eucalyptus leaves are poisonous to most animals. The koala can eat them only because it has specially helpful microbes, called bacteria, in its digestive system. These break down the poison into harmless substances. The microbes came originally from the koala's mother, in her special droppings or "pap" that it ate as a baby.

Eucalyptus leaves take a long time to digest and do not contain many nutrients or much energy. This low-energy food is one reason why the koala spends most of its time asleep, moves slowly, and rarely travels far.

◄ Koalas sleep during the hottest part of the day. They find somewhere quiet and shady, then rest until the heat passes.

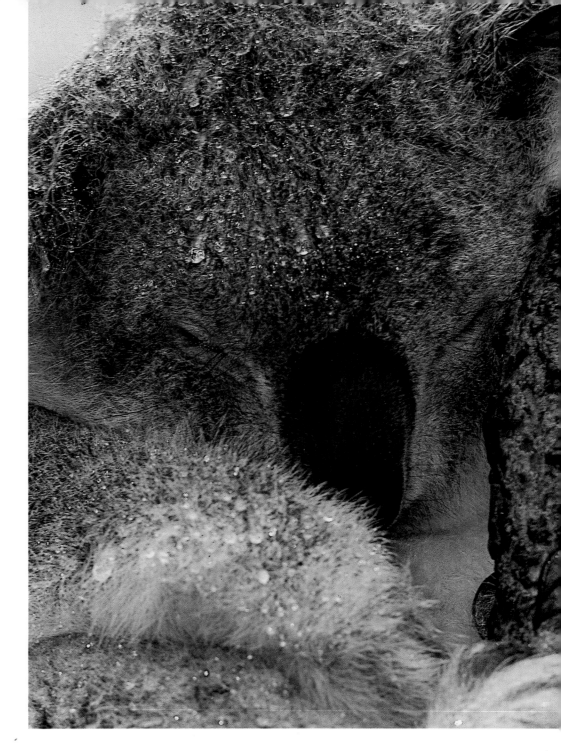

▶ In wet weather koalas curl up and keep still. Their oily fur keeps out even the heaviest rain, and the koalas stay warm and dry.

Useful Oils

Eucalyptus leaves contain large amounts of oils. These are taken into the koala's body, and then ooze out through the skin. They make a koala smell strongly of eucalyptus. The oil also makes the furry coat waterproof. Even during heavy storms, raindrops run off instead of soaking into the fur and skin.

Climbing

Each of the koala's hands and feet has five digits. The hands have three digits in the usual position, like our fingers, but the other two are on the side. So a koala seems to have two thumbs. This gives a strong, hook-like grip. Both hands and feet have pads of very rough skin, for extra grip.

▲ A koala's hand

▶ A koala's foot

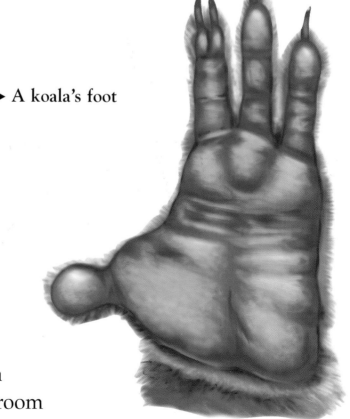

Each finger and toe, except for the big toe, has a long, sharp claw. The second and third toes are joined together, making these two claws very close. This forms a comb that the koala uses to groom or clean its fur.

NO DRINK

The name "koala" comes from a native Australian word meaning "no-drink."

▲ All plants contain water, but it can be difficult to reach. The koalas' slow and efficient digestive system absorbs all moisture from its food.

Drinking

All animals must have water. Leaves contain large amounts of moisture, and a koala gets more than two-thirds of the water it needs directly from its food. This is topped off by rain and dew on the leaves and branches. The koala is also efficient at saving body water. It avoids hot sunshine and does not sweat. This is why koalas very rarely need to drink. They may lap from a pool in times of drought, when the leaves contain less water than usual.

Adult Life

Home ranges of koalas often overlap. A male koala is more active than a female, and usually he has a bigger home range. Indeed, it may include the ranges of three or four females. But these neighbors rarely meet each other. Koalas are solitary animals. They hear, see, and smell others nearby— and avoid them. They live peacefully like this throughout most of the year.

◄ This male koala is using his loud bellow call to warn rivals to stay away.

BIGGER MALE

Male koalas are much larger than females. For their size, they also have broader chests and faces.

During the breeding season, between September and March, male koalas get very aggressive. They try to become the chief or dominant male of the area. Only the dominant male can mate with the females. The males call out at night with powerful grunts and bellows. The sounds tell other males to keep away, and also attract females. Each male judges the size and power of his rivals by the amount of noise they make. Often a young or small male hears the loud growls of a larger male nearby, and keeps quiet.

▲ Males sometimes leave the safety of trees and wander around in search of females.

Fighting

If male koalas do not drive away rivals by calling, they may fight to become dominant. They chase around the trees, biting and scratching. They might wrestle as each tries to push the opponent out of the tree. When two males are evenly matched, the battle can be long and vicious. Injuries are common and even deaths occur.

The winner becomes the dominant male and mates with all the females in the area. To mark his area, or territory, he rubs against the trees, to smear on a strong-smelling oil from his chest gland. This warns other males that the territory is already taken.

▲ Male koalas occasionally fight for the right to mate. The resulting injuries show that these animals are not the soft, cuddly creatures that many people believe.

▶ A male koala clearly shows the scent gland in the center of his chest. This is used to mark his territory with a strong smell that warns rivals to keep away.

A dominant male usually holds his position for a few years. As he gets older, he is driven out by a younger, stronger rival. Young males are big enough to compete at about four years of age. Until then, they keep clear of the fighting. Some smaller males never become dominant and will never breed. Dominance is important only during the breeding season. For the rest of the year, males do not call or fight.

FEARFUL SCREAM

Koalas have a "fear-call" they make when frightened. It sounds like a human baby screaming.

▲ Males and females stay together only long enough to mate. The male then moves away in search of other females.

Breeding

When a female koala reaches the age of 2 years, she is ready to mate. Males can mate when they are about 4 years old. As the breeding season arrives, and nearby males make their deep, roaring grunts, she replies with her own call to attract them. The male approaches, but he must wait until the female allows him to mate. If he tries too soon, she drives him away with bites and scratches. Most matings take place at night.

SHORTER LIVES

Male koalas usually die earlier than females. They can be badly injured when fighting. Also, they travel farther on the ground, and so they risk attack by predators.

▼ Some eucalyptus trees produce a gas that burns well, so forest fires in Australia can often travel quickly. Bush fires are one of the biggest killers of koalas, because the animals cannot move fast enough to avoid the approaching flames.

A female koala may live for 12 years and produce around six joeys. She does not give birth every year, especially if there is a drought or a serious forest fire. There is no point in breeding if her young would have little chance of survival. Also, caring for a joey makes her life slightly more dangerous. She must drink more than other koalas, because extra moisture is needed to produce milk. This brings the mother down from the trees, in search of pools and streams. On the ground, she is at greater risk from predators.

Threats

Australia once had huge forests of eucalyptus trees, where koalas were common and widespread. Native aboriginal people hunted them, but never killed enough to threaten their survival.

European settlers arrived in the 18th century. They soon began to hunt koalas for food, because they were easy to kill. Then koalas were also hunted for their thick, warm fur. This was sold abroad at high prices, often as "wombat fur." In the early 1900s, up to 30,000 koala furs each year were sent to London alone. Many more were shipped to the rest of Europe and North America.

▼ The red fox is not a native Australian animal, but was brought over from Europe by early settlers. Foxes are now thriving in the wild and are one of the major killers of koalas.

▲ A conservation poster showing koalas moving in and taking over a house belonging to a logger.

Habitat Destruction

European settlers also cleared vast areas of eucalyptus woodland to plant crops and graze farm animals. Four-fifths of the original eucalyptus woods disappeared. The koala rapidly became a rare species. In 1927, the Australian government passed a law forbidding the export of koala furs. But many people still hunted them for food.

FIRST SIGHTING

The first recorded sighting of a koala by a European settler was on January 26, 1798, by Englishman John Price. He was a servant of the Governor of Australia.

Saving Koalas

By 1930, koalas were so rare that animal experts believed the species could disappear altogether. The government made new laws to protect it. Large-scale hunting was completely banned.

Koalas in South Australia had already been wiped out. Conservation workers launched projects to bring them back to areas where they once lived. Koalas living farther north were caught and released into suitable woodlands in the south. These re-introductions worked well and the koalas bred successfully. Thanks to legal protection and good conservation, the koala is no longer a threatened species except in some small areas.

▼ In a koala hospital, an injured animal is fed before being returned to the wild.

Still a Major Problem

Protecting the koala means protecting its habitat too. Every year, more eucalyptus woodland is cut down for farmland or human settlements. Without such woods, koalas cannot survive. Most live outside national parks, where woodlands have less protection. As a wood becomes smaller, the koalas are trapped in the few remaining trees. Youngsters looking for new home ranges have nowhere to go. If they are not rescued, they die. Habitat destruction is still a major problem for koalas and other wildlife.

▲ Five captive koalas share a branch. Wild koalas are not normally so tolerant of each other.

Captive Koalas

Koalas can be moved around Australia, provided they are taken to suitable eucalyptus habitats. However, very few have survived in other countries. From about 1800, many were captured and sold to zoos overseas, but unfortunately, most died within a few weeks. Today, only about ten zoos and nature parks outside Australia have koalas.

▲Visitors stroking a koala at a zoo in Australia.

In Australia, koalas are enormously popular. They are a major attraction for tourists from all over the world. Since they try to stay in one home range for life, they are fairly easy to keep in nature parks and zoos. Koalas do not need cages or fences. They wander freely among the eucalyptus trees. They could easily leave, but as long as there is plenty of food, they stay in one place—just as they do in the wild.

OFFICIAL ANIMAL

The koala is the official animal emblem of Australia's northeast state, Queensland.

▼ Koalas often come down to the ground at night and many are accidentally killed by traffic. This sign warns drivers to be careful.

YEARLY DEATHS

Each year up to 4,000 koalas are killed by dogs and road traffic.

KOALAS
CROSS HERE
AT
NIGHT

KOALAS CROSSING

Koala Life Cycle

 1 > A newborn koala, or joey, is tiny and helpless. It weighs just one-hundredth of an ounce (0.5 g) and is smaller than your thumb.

< 2  For the first few months the joey stays inside its mother's pouch, feeding on her milk. The pouch entrance remains closed.

 3 > By the age of 5 months, the joey's eyes are open and it can look out of the pouch. It still stays there and feeds on its mother's milk.

 **4** The joey leaves its mother's pouch for the first time at about 6 months old. It gradually moves farther, but it dashes back to the pouch if danger threatens. It feeds on its mother's special droppings, called "pap."

 5 At 9 months old, the young koala is too big for its mother's pouch and rides on her back. By the age of 1 year, the koala is ready to leave its mother and find its own home range.

 **6** Female koalas start to breed at the age of 2 years. Males usually begin at 4 years. In the wild, koalas live for up to 12 years. On average, females live longer than males.

Glossary

Breed To produce young.

Camouflage (KAM-uh-flahzh) The color or pattern of an animal that helps it to blend in with its surroundings.

Dominant (DOM-uh-nuhnt) The leading animal in a group or area, usually the most powerful and aggressive.

Habitat (HAB-uh-tat) An animal or plant's natural place.

Home range (RAYNJ) An area of land used by an animal (or group), where the animal lives and finds all its food.

Incisors (in-SIZ-urz) Sharp cutting teeth at the front of the mouth.

Joey (JOH-ee) A young koala.

Marsupial (mar-SOO-pee-uhl) A mammal that keeps and feeds its young in a pouch.

Molars (MOH-lurz) Flat teeth at the back of the mouth, used for grinding and chewing.

Nocturnal (nok-TUR-nuhl) Active at night or in darkness.

Pap Special droppings produced by a mother koala to feed her baby.

Predator (PRED-uh-tur) An animal that kills and eats other creatures.

Suckle (SUHK-uhl) To drink milk from a mother mammal's teats (nipples).

Territory (TER-uh-tor-ee) An area that is controlled and defended by an animal or group.

Threatened (THRET-uhnd) A species whose numbers are low and is in danger of extinction (disappearing completely).

Weaning (WEEN-ing) To stop drinking mother's milk and start eating solid food.

Further Information

Organizations to Contact

World Wildlife Fund
1250 24th Street, N.W.
Washington, D.C. 20037

The Wilderness Society
130 Davey Street,
Hobart, Tasmania 700
Australia
Website:
www.wilderness.org.au

Websites

www.koala.net
Run by the Lone Pine Koala
Sanctuary, the world's largest
collection of koalas. Lots of
pictures, information, and links.

www.thekoala.com
Plenty of information,
pictures, and links.

www.australianwildlife.com.au
Information on Australian
wildlife and conservation.

Books to Read

Smith-Saunders, Gail. *Animals Growing and Changing: Koalas.* Dover, NH: Pebble Books, 1997.

Sotzek, Hannelore. *Crabapples: The Koala Is Not a Bear!* New York: Crabtree Publishing, 1997.

Theodorou, Rod. *Animals in Danger: Koala.* Chicago, IL: Heinemann Library, 2001.

Index

Page numbers in **bold** refer to photographs or illustrations.